A Sudoku Puzzle-Setter's Guide to

CREATE CLASSIC
SUDOKU

Make Your Own in Minutes

YALING ZHENG, PhD

Editing by Amy Hill and John Humpert
Cover design by Lisa Von De Linde

www.createclassicsudoku.com

ISBN-10:   0-9962-0420-2
ISBN-13: 978-0-9962042-0-0

DEDICATION

To my parents, my daughters, and my husband.

ACKNOWLEDGMENTS

Writing a book is a team effort. I have been fortunate!

I am blessed to work with the very talented Amy Hill, whose questions, tips, and inspirations helped me to express my ideas and techniques clearly. Without her, this book could not exist. I appreciate the brilliant editing touch by John Humpert. I am thankful for Allison Yeager, Elaine Hackett, and Mike Bacha, whose diligent reviews were most helpful.

I am grateful for my excellent book cover designer, Marianne Nowicki. Also, I thank Susan Gertz, Brian Heim, Kristin Johnson, Sharareh Khosravani, Zoe Liang, and Marianne Nowicki for their design ideas.

And for all your patience with me, I cannot thank my spouse and my daughters enough! I know at times, it seems that the act of writing places its demands not only on me but also on you who are closest to me. I also want to thank my parents for your unchanging love and constant encouragement.

CONTENTS

PREFACE

Logic-lovers everywhere, from age 10 to 100—whether young and curious or mature and motivated—welcome! Logic comes into play not only in computer technology and science fiction but also throughout our lives.

In 2003, as a graduate student in a computer science at the University of Nebraska, I picked Sudoku puzzles to be the focus of some of my projects. This choice led me to a great appreciation for the elegance, the "rhyme and reason" in the logic, and the accessibility of that elegance as we dive into the craft of Sudoku puzzle-setting. What intrigued me most? I noticed that technology is not essential—yes, faster and efficient, but not essential—for making a classic Sudoku. From that point on, I have felt challenged to share this elegance for the benefit of everyone interested.

This may be the first book to explain how to manually make Sudoku puzzles using basic logical reasoning techniques, so read on! Study the easy procedures and use the special techniques to become a very good puzzle-setter. As you read, follow along and actively practice in your own grids (see the back of the book). Within a morning or an afternoon, you can manually create your first Sudoku puzzles!

1 – BASICS

I believe that everyone with even just a mild interest in logic can become a good Sudoku puzzle-setter. Beginners can use this chapter to "get up to speed." Not a beginner? Then you can skip to Chapter 2.

What is a Sudoku? It is a puzzle about logic not math. A typical Sudoku is a big box that holds nine mid-size boxes (thick lines) that in turn hold nine squares (thin lines).

As seen in newspapers and magazines, a ready-to-solve Sudoku puzzle comes to us with some squares pre-filled with single-digit numbers. A puzzle solvers' mission: Place numbers in the remaining boxes—*correctly!* A classic Sudoku has just one solution. Solving may be easy or difficult. Why is that? Stay tuned!

How do we fill it? In a correctly solved puzzle...

- Rows (across) will each hold ...   numbers **1** to **9**
- Columns (down) will each hold...   numbers **1** to **9**
- Boxes (thick lines) will each hold... numbers **1** to **9**

In other words, each number, from **1** to **9**, will appear exactly one time in each row, exactly one time in each column, and exactly one time in each mid-size, 3-by-3 box bounded by thick lines.

> **Will this book help readers SOLVE better or faster?** Probably yes, but keep in mind please that my main purpose is to show that **you can manually MAKE a Sudoku.** Read on, gain skills as a competent puzzle-setter and, likely, you'll become a sharper puzzle-solver too.

Classic Sudoku

What is special about a classic Sudoku puzzle? Two things: As mentioned, a classic Sudoku has one and only one solution. **Only one possible number fits correctly in each square.** Also, whether right-side up or upside-down, the **arrangement of pre-filled squares is the same.** This is known as *180-degree rotational symmetry*. Got that? Let's view an example of a classic Sudoku.

A Classic Sudoku Puzzle

	5			8	3			
	8	7	1	4		9		
6	4		5		9	3		
8	7		9		4	2	5	
	5		6		8		1	
	1	9	3		2		7	6
		4	2		1		3	8
		2		3	5	7	6	
			4	6		1		

I will mention it again later, but it's worth noting now that a *classic* Sudoku puzzle will have the same *arrangement* of squares pre-filled, whether right-side up or upside-down.

Rows, columns, boxes—and diagonals

We need to name the different parts of the main big box in order to talk about them. Thus…

- **R** will stand for row (straight across, side to side)
- **C** will stand for column (from up to down, vertical)
- **B** will stand for box—referring to the mid-size boxes, and
- **D** will stand for diagonal—of which there are only two.

Rows are named **R1**, **R2**, **R3**, …all the way to **R9**.

Names of Rows

Note: As an example, Row 3 — **R3** — is in gray.

R1→		5		8	3			
R2→	8	7	1	4		9		
R3→ 6	4		5		9	3		
8	7		9		4	2	5	
	5		6		8		1	
	1	9	3		2		7	6
		4	2		1		3	8
		2		3	5	7	6	
R9→			4	6		1		

Columns are named **C1**, **C2**, **C3**, ... to **C9**.

Names of Columns

Note: As an example, Column 3 — **C3** — is in gray.

C1	C2	C3	...	...	...	...	...	C9
		5		8	3			
	8	7	1	4		9		
6	4		5		9	3		
8	7		9		4	2	5	
	5		6		8		1	
	1	9	3		2		7	6
		4	2		1		3	8
		2		3	5	7	6	
			4	6		1		

Boxes are named **B1, B2, B3,** …through **B9**. The box names are arranged just like the numbers on a telephone dial pad.

Names of Boxes

Note: As an example, Box 3 — **B3** — is in gray.

B1	B2	B3
B4	B5	B6
B7	B8	B9

Diagonals: The two diagonal are **D1** and **D2**. The first, **D1**, runs from top left to bottom right. Conversely, its opposite, **D2**, runs from top right to bottom left. The square in the center is midpoint of both **D1** and **D2**.

Names of Diagonals

Note: Center square **R5C5** is located in both **D1** and **D2**.

Constraints

A constraint is just a rule stating that each single-digit number from **1** to **9** will occur only once per row, per column, and per box.

Row constraint. Numbers **1** to **9** will fit only one time per row. In the example below, we can use row constraint to *infer*—that is, to reach a conclusion based on the set of facts that rule out all other possibilities—that only **9** will fit in R1C9 (gray square at top right).

Visual Examples of Constraints

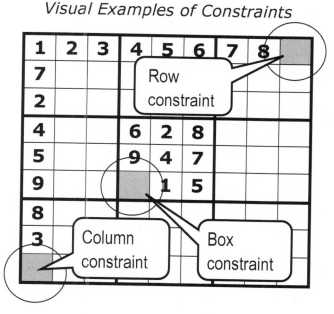

Column constraint. Numbers **1** to **9** will also be used only one time per column. In the example above, column constraint allows us to infer that only **6** can fit in R9C1 (gray square at bottom left).

Box constraint. Numbers **1** to **9** will also be used only one time per box. In the example above, box constraint allows us to infer that inside B5, the square R6C4 (in the box in the center) can be filled only with the number **3**.

Note: There is no such thing as "diagonal constraint."

2 – QUICK TOUR OF CHALLENGES

In the following overview, I introduce some considerations that I think you will find interesting about puzzle-setting.

Tip #1: Choose to make your puzzle a classic

What kind of Sudoku should I make? You want to make a classic Sudoku, which provides puzzle-solvers a partially completed grid that meets *two conditions*: (1) the puzzle has just one possible solution, and (2) it exhibits 180-degree rotational symmetry. More on this shortly.

What will be our basic approach to manually make a Sudoku puzzle? It is a simple two-stage process.

1. Make a fully completed grid using special techniques.
2. Remove numbers from the grid.

First topic: Fully completed grids.

Tip #2: Fill grids using approaches I show you

Why do I need guidance on how to fill a grid? Can't I just "do it my way," starting to set numbers in squares any way I like? Well, you COULD take a 9-x-9 blank grid and start filling it in as you like, placing numbers **1** to **9** in rows, columns, and boxes while avoiding all repetition but then don't say I didn't warn you! This random approach can require hours to generate a valid Sudoku puzzle. There IS a *tiny* chance that you could get lucky. The result? Your randomly-generated Sudoku may have *no* solution or *many* solutions. We want our puzzles to have *just one* possible solution, that is, we want numbers to fit in squares in only one possible successful arrangement. The reality is that even after hundreds of attempts based just on impulse, you may wind up with zero usable puzzles. Don't worry, there is a better way!

So wait a minute! Couldn't we recycle and re-use newspapers' and magazines' puzzle solution grids? Technically, yes, you could, and if you insist on that approach, you can skip to Chapter 5 now. Come back to this chapter when ready to look into the "rhyme and reason" of creating your own grids.

Making a fully completed grid

The next two chapters present techniques to create fully completed grids manually. Also Chapter 6 presents a start-to-finish example. Alternatively, you can use software employing a *backtracking algorithm.*

Backtracking sounds like fun. Can I try it manually? I suggest No, don't. Backtracking is a "trial and error" method for finding solutions to Sudoku puzzle problems. In this approach, starting with a blank grid, you place numbers to fill the grid and when a placement doesn't work then you try a different number. You would repeat the procedure until you fill all squares. Two problems here:

1. As one gets deeply involved in backtracking, trying various numbers for each square, one's later progress relies on a lot of memorization of earlier steps.

2. Manual backtracking takes time and will make mighty demands upon your attention span and ability to memorize.

Removing numbers from a grid

With a fully completed grid in hand, we will use techniques that I introduce in Chapter 5 to remove numbers, to guarantee that your result will be a classic puzzle.

Tell me a little more about the nature of a classic puzzle. It will meet TWO CONDITIONS.

- Your classic puzzle will have only one possible solution, thus your future puzzle solvers will be able to infer numbers using known, logical solving techniques.
- Your classic puzzle will, when rotated 180 degrees, show the same squares pre-filled. So when you see whether you can clear a number from **R1C9**, for example, you must also check on **R9C1**, its 180-degree symmetrical counterpart.

Can we see a quick example of how to begin to remove numbers? Yes. Start with a fully completed grid.

A Fully Completed Sudoku Grid

4	9	8	7	3	6	1	5	2
1	5	2	4	8	9	3	7	6
6	7	3	5	1	2	8	9	4
9	1	6	8	4	7	2	3	5
5	3	7	2	6	1	9	4	8
8	2	4	3	9	5	6	1	7
7	8	9	6	5	3	4	2	1
3	6	5	1	2	4	7	8	9
2	4	1	9	7	8	5	6	3

We can remove numbers in **R1C9** and **R9C1**, thus our grid contains two cleared squares.

Grid with 2 Cleared Squares

4	9	8	7	3	6	1	5	
1	5	2	4	8	9	3	7	6
6	7	3	5	1	2	8	9	4
9	1	6	8	4	7	2	3	5
5	3	7	2	6	1	9	4	8
8	2	4	3	9	5	6	1	7
7	8	9	6	5	3	4	2	1
3	6	5	1	2	4	7	8	9
	4	1	9	7	8	5	6	3

Future puzzle-solvers will now be able to infer how to complete the puzzle. The table shows the solution path.

At...	Fill in...	As allowed by ...
R1C9	2	*In each case:*
R9C1	2	Row constraint, column constraint, and/or box constraint

Safety first!

Please realize that as we clear squares, we do so only because tests that we are conducting (in our heads at least) ensure that our future puzzle-solvers can find their way. We can *safely* remove numbers "permanently" only if tests pass. When a test fails, it just means that we know no safe way to clear. So we move on, selecting and testing a different pair. (Remember the nature of a classic puzzle and the important two conditions?) Let's examine whether we can also clear the pair R3C2 and R7C8.

Grid with 4 Cleared Squares

4	9	8	7	3	6	1	5	
1	5	2	4	8	9	3	7	6
6		3	5	1	2	8	9	4
9	1	6	8	4	7	2	3	5
5	3	7	2	6	1	9	4	8
8	2	4	3	9	5	6	1	7
7	8	9	6	5	3	4		1
3	6	5	1	2	4	7	8	9
	4	1	9	7	8	5	6	3

Our Sudoku puzzle now has four cleared squares. Can future puzzle-solvers infer how to complete the puzzle? Let's double-check. The table shows the solution path.

At...	Fill in...	As allowed by ...
R3C2	7	*In each case:* Row constraint, column constraint, and/or box constraint
R7C8	2	
R1C9	2	
R9C1	2	

All is well. It is safe to clear squares R3C2 and R7C8.

Now I know how to begin to clear a grid, but how will I know when to stop? Keep testing and clearing pairs of numbers until you cannot find a pair of squares whose numbers can be safely removed.

Tip #3: Go easy on yourself about puzzle difficulty

As you might imagine, creating an easy Sudoku takes less time than creating a highly challenging puzzle. Beginning puzzle-setters should manage expectations about creating very difficult puzzles and set goals to create puzzles that beginning and intermediate puzzle-solvers can appreciate. As you "delve deeper," you will find my guidance to you is:

- *thorough* for successful creation of easy puzzles and
- *sufficient* for pointing you in the right directions if you wish to go on to create advanced-level puzzles.

Meanwhile, let me share some considerations that I think are important.

Considerations about "easy" and "difficult"

Let's zip our lips about a puzzle's difficulty level. It's probably better if puzzle-solvers know nothing of our own opinions of our own puzzles. Let them see for themselves. Chances are, while solving, they will focus mainly on "getting to the finish line." After that, they remember only how much fun they had.

Solvers' mistakes work both FOR and AGAINST us: Most mistakes lead puzzle-solvers into trouble but, interestingly, some mistakes wind up as correct guesses that lead to quick success. In other words, *unlucky mistakes* can make simple puzzles difficult or impossible; while a *lucky mistake* can turn a difficult puzzle into child's play. When, where, and how mistakes happen are completely beyond our control. Just enjoy the surprises!

If creating a difficult puzzle is still your goal, then study advanced techniques independently (in this book, I *mention* some but I will not *go into detail* about them). Apply them near the end of your puzzle-setting effort when simpler techniques won't clear any more pairs of squares. In other words, for puzzle-setting, it is best to use easier techniques as long as we can and avoid using advanced techniques until we "must"—if at all.

Again, it's beyond our control how puzzle-solvers rate our puzzles' difficulty so let's not worry. When our puzzle-solvers *don't know* what we know, this tends to work in our favor. Levels of difficulty can be overrated. And let's not forget: It's generally good to give our puzzle-solvers a challenge with which they can be victorious.

More discussions about puzzle difficulty are in the second half of Chapter 4 and the first part of Chapter 5, where I mention another author's book to point you in a great direction if you wish to "go there."

To repeat: All in all, you will find here sufficient direction to create puzzles at the level of challenge and difficulty that appeal to you most. In order to create puzzles at higher levels of difficulty, *read carefully* and *think for yourself* about the directions in which I point. And enjoy!

3 – FILL A GRID

As you have seen, our basic approach to manually create a Sudoku puzzle is a two-stage process:

1. <u>Make a fully completed grid using special techniques.</u> ⟵
2. Remove numbers from the grid.

To ease into the first stage, let us start with a few easy *exercises.* By the way, all of these exercises are closely related—remember R (row), C (column) and B (box)? This goes for Exercise 3 too, with its three approaches: All are closely related.

Exercise 1: Introduction to group filling

One row at a time, we will fill in numbers **1** to **9**. We will do this nine times for nine rows.

Exercise 1 is much simpler than generating a fully completed grid because our only focus is to fill each row with single digits while we honor row constraint. That's all. Forget about column constraint and box constraint for now. Exercise 1 is just for warming up and getting a better understanding of what we're doing.

Begin with a blank grid, and when you fill a row, make sure you fill it with nine different numbers **1** to **9** in order to satisfy row constraint. Below are some examples.

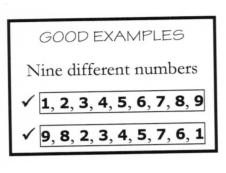

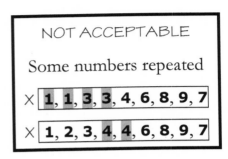

Fill each row with any sequence of nine different numbers. To satisfy row constraint, be sure to not repeat numbers, just like in "Good Examples," above.

Below is an example Step 1 for starting Exercise 1.

Step 1	Fill R1 with numbers **1, 2, 3, 4, 5, 6, 7, 8, 9**.

In carrying out Step 1 above, you would create a partially filled grid that would now look like this.

After Exercise 1, Step 1

1	2	3	4	5	6	7	8	9

Note that you can fill **R1** with ANY sequence of nine different single digits. For example, you could have also started out this way...

Fill **R1** with numbers **4**, **3**, **1**, **9**, **6**, **7**, **2**, **5**, **8**.

...or this way...

Fill **R1** with numbers **6**, **9**, **7**, **2**, **5**, **8**, **1**, **4**, **3**.

Let's view more example steps for finishing Exercise 1.

Step 2	Fill R2 with numbers **2**, **3**, **4**, **5**, **6**, **7**, **8**, **9**, **1**.

In carrying out Step 2 above, you would create a partially filled grid that would now look like this.

After Exercise 1, Step 2

1	2	3	4	5	6	7	8	9
2	3	4	5	6	7	8	9	1

Let's continue with more steps.

Step 3	Fill R3 with numbers **3, 4, 5, 6, 7, 8, 9, 1, 2**.
Step 4	Fill R4 with numbers **4, 5, 6, 7, 8, 9, 1, 2, 3**.
Step 5	Fill R5 with numbers **5, 3, 7, 2, 6, 1, 9, 4, 8**.
Step 6	Fill R6 with numbers **8, 2, 4, 3, 9, 5, 6, 1, 7**.
Step 7	Fill R7 with numbers **7, 8, 9, 6, 5, 3, 4, 2, 1**.
Step 8	Fill R8 with numbers **3, 6, 5, 1, 2, 4, 7, 8, 9**.
Step 9	Fill R9 with numbers **2, 4, 1, 9, 7, 8, 5, 6, 3**.

In carrying out step 1–9 above, you would create a fully completed grid that would now look like this.

Completed Practice Grid after Exercise 1

1	2	3	4	5	6	7	8	9
2	3	4	5	6	7	8	9	1
3	4	5	6	7	8	9	1	2
4	5	6	7	8	9	1	2	3
5	3	7	2	6	1	9	4	8
8	2	4	3	9	5	6	1	7
7	8	9	6	5	3	4	2	1
3	6	5	1	2	4	7	8	9
2	4	1	9	7	8	5	6	3

So let's now review: To complete Exercise 1, we filled one row and then another, continuing until all rows were filled.

In this approach, we effectively split Exercise 1 into nine sub-tasks, whereby each sub-task was to fill a row.

We will call this technique *group filling*, and we can use it to fill rows, columns, or boxes strategically.

- *Group filling by row* is about filling each *row* with nine different numbers **1** to **9**.

- *Group filling by column* is about filling each *column* with nine different numbers **1** to **9**.

- *Group filling by box* is about filling each *box* with nine different numbers **1** to **9**.

Whichever group filling approach you use, ***continue the same approach*** to complete Exercise 1. And let's not forget: Exercise 1 only demonstrates group filling; we won't try to use it to create a useful puzzle. Now on to Exercise 2, which is more challenging.

Exercise 2: Introduction to circular shifting

Again, one row at a time, we will fill in numbers **1** to **9**. We will do this nine times for nine rows. With Exercise 2, we come closer to actual basic puzzle-setting but we won't arrive just yet. Here is an example Step 1 for this exercise.

Step 1	Fill **R1** with numbers **1**, **2**, **3**, **4**, **5**, **6**, **7**, **8**, **9**.

In carrying out Step 1 above, you would create a partially filled grid that would now look like this.

After Exercise 2, Step 1

1	2	3	4	5	6	7	8	9

Note that you can fill **R1** with any sequence of nine different single digits, same as in Exercise 1. But here in Exercise 2, as we begin to fill **R2**, we take column constraint also into consideration. We will use a ***circular shift*** to do the deed. It's not too difficult. Let's have a look.

IF we start with a sequence like this:

$$\{1, 2, 3, 4, 5, 6, 7, 8, 9\},$$

- THEN a circular shift ***by ONE slot*** looks like this:

- AND a circular shift ***by TWO slots*** looks like this:

- AND a circular shift ***by THREE slots*** looks like this:

With the arrows and the shifts in spacing in the lines above, perhaps you can easily see how the four sequences are different from but related to each other. Circular shift is easy, right?

So if we "circular-shift" Step 1's sequence by one slot and put the result in **R2**, look! We meet column constraint!

| Step 2 | Fill **R2** with a circular shift of the sequence of numbers in **R1** by ONE slot. |

In carrying out Step 2 above, you would create a partially filled grid that would now look like this.

After Exercise 2, Step 2

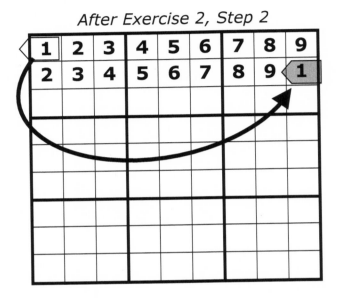

Did you think about this? We could in fact satisfy the column constraint with a circular shift of the sequence in **R1** by *two, three, four, five, six, seven,* or *eight* slots and put any of those results in **R2**. But anyhow, let's continue.

Step 3	Fill **R3** with a circular shift of the sequence of numbers in **R2** by ONE slot.
Step 4	Fill **R4** with a circular shift of the sequence of numbers in **R3** by ONE slot.
Step 5	Fill **R5** with a circular shift of the sequence of numbers in **R4** by ONE slot.

Step 6	Fill R6 with a circular shift of the sequence of numbers in R5 by ONE slot.
Step 7	Fill R7 with a circular shift of the sequence of numbers in R6 by ONE slot.
Step 8	Fill R8 with a circular shift of the sequence of numbers in R7 by ONE slot.
Step 9	Fill R9 with a circular shift of the sequence of numbers in R8 by ONE slot.

Now, we have a completed grid for Exercise 2.

Completed Practice Grid after Exercise 2

1	2	3	4	5	6	7	8	9
2	3	4	5	6	7	8	9	1
3	4	5	6	7	8	9	1	2
4	5	6	7	8	9	1	2	3
5	6	7	8	9	1	2	3	4
6	7	8	9	1	2	3	4	5
7	8	9	1	2	3	4	5	6
8	9	1	2	3	4	5	6	7
9	1	2	3	4	5	6	7	8

Note that all possible circular shifts of the sequence of {**1**, **2**, **3**, **4**, **5**, **6**, **7**, **8**, **9**} were each used just one time. Also recall that we used TWO grid-filling techniques in Exercise 2: *group filling* and *circular shift*. Now, on to our next exercise—which is a bit more challenging. Ready?

Exercise 3: Running with all three constraints

Again we fill boxes with digits—one row at a time, nine times for nine rows—but this time we add one more consideration to create fully completed grids as promised.

Using group filling and circular shift still, as we fill by row for example, we must now watch column constraint AND box constraint too. Previously we had only watched column constraint. To show all three approaches for group filling, I have prepared exercises: "3R," "3C," and "3BX."

"Row, row, row" approach ("Exercise 3R")

Here is an example Step 1 for starting Exercise 3R.

Step 1	Fill **R1** with nine different numbers **1**, **2**, **3**, **4**, **5**, **6**, **7**, **8**, **9**.

In carrying out Step 1 above, we create a partially filled grid like this, with **R1** filled. As always, we can fill **R1** with any sequence of different digits, as explained in Exercise 1.

After Step 1   Exercise "3R"

1	2	3	4	5	6	7	8	9

Let's continue.

Step 2	Fill **R2** with a circular shift of the sequence of numbers in **R1** by THREE slots.

Analysis for Step 2: When we fill **R2**, can we fill it with a circular shift of the sequence of **R1** by ONE slot to satisfy both column and box constraint? No, column constraint would be fine, but box constraint would be broken.

- What if we circular-shift the sequence of **R1** by TWO slots to fill **R2**? This also would satisfy only column constraint but not box constraint.

- What if we circular-shift the sequence of **R1** by THREE slots to fill **R2**? Great! THIS satisfies BOTH column constraint and box constraint!

Alternatively, we could circular-shift the sequence of **R1** by SIX slots to fill **R2**. In steps that follow, however, I can only show and explain one circular shift sequence. Still, feel free to explore possibilities! After completing Step 2, our grid now looks like this, with **R2** filled.

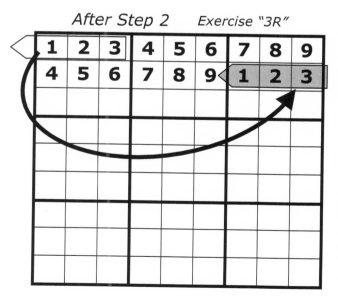

After Step 2   *Exercise "3R"*

Now we repeat for **R3** what we did for **R2**: Circular-shift the sequence of the previous row by THREE slots.

Step 3	Fill **R3** with a circular shift of the sequence of numbers in **R2** by THREE slots.

In carrying out Step 3 above, we create a partially filled grid that now looks like this, with **R3** filled.

After Step 3   Exercise "3R"

1	2	3	4	5	6	7	8	9
4	5	6	7	8	9	1	2	3
7	8	9	1	2	3	4	5	6

Let's continue.

So wait a minute! If we continue to circular-shift the same number of slots every time now, won't we run into constraint trouble? Yes, exactly right. It's time right now to make a change in order to avoid any trouble with constraints! Pay attention carefully in the next step.

Step 4	Fill **R4** with a circular shift of the sequence of numbers in **R3** by ONE slot.

Analysis for Step 4: When we fill **R4**, can we fill it with a circular shift of the sequence in **R3** by three slots? No, if we fill **R4** with sequence {**1**, **2**, **3**, **4**, **5**, **6**, **7**, **8**, **9**}, then we would violate the column constraint.

- What if we fill **R4** with a circular shift of the sequence in **R3** by ONE slot? Yes, we can do that.

You may want to try the circular shift of the sequence in **R3** by *two, four, five, seven,* or *eight* slots— as long as it does not violate row, column, and box constraints.

In carrying out Step 1 above, we create a partially filled grid that now looks like this, with **R4** filled.

After Step 4   Exercise "3R"

1	2	3	4	5	6	7	8	9
4	5	6	7	8	9	1	2	3
7	8	9	1	2	3	4	5	6
8	9	1	2	3	4	5	6	7

Why change our circular shifting from THREE slots to just ONE here? It's a way to respect all three (**R**, **C**, and **B**) constraints!

Let's continue.

| Step 5 | Fill **R5** with a circular shift of the sequence of numbers in **R4** by THREE slots. |

Analysis for Step 5: When we fill **R5**, can we fill it with a circular shift of the sequence of **R4** by ONE slot? No, because that would violate the box constraint.

So, what if we fill **R5** with a circular shift of the sequence of **R4** by THREE slots? Yes, that works.

After Step 5   *Exercise "3R"*

1	2	3	4	5	6	7	8	9
4	5	6	7	8	9	1	2	3
7	8	9	1	2	3	4	5	6
8	9	1	2	3	4	5	6	7
2	3	4	5	6	7	8	9	1

Now we repeat for **R6** what we did for **R5**.

| Step 6 | Fill **R6** with a circular shift of the sequence of numbers in **R5** by THREE slots. |

After Step 6   Exercise "3R"

1	2	3	4	5	6	7	8	9
4	5	6	7	8	9	1	2	3
7	8	9	1	2	3	4	5	6
8	9	1	2	3	4	5	6	7
2	3	4	5	6	7	8	9	1
5	6	7	8	9	1	2	3	4

Now we repeat for **R7** what we did for **R4**.

Step 7	Fill **R7** with a circular shift of the sequence of numbers in **R6** by ONE slot.

After Step 7   Exercise "3R"

1	2	3	4	5	6	7	8	9
4	5	6	7	8	9	1	2	3
7	8	9	1	2	3	4	5	6
8	9	1	2	3	4	5	6	7
2	3	4	5	6	7	8	9	1
5	6	7	8	9	1	2	3	4
6	7	8	9	1	2	3	4	5

Change from THREE slots to just ONE here to respect all three constraints!

Now we repeat for **R8** what we did for both **R2** and **R5**.

Step 8	Fill **R8** with a circular shift of the sequence of numbers in **R7** by THREE slots.

In carrying out Step 8 above, we create a partially filled grid that now looks like this, with **R8** filled.

After Step 8   Exercise "3R"

1	2	3	4	5	6	7	8	9
4	5	6	7	8	9	1	2	3
7	8	9	1	2	3	4	5	6
8	9	1	2	3	4	5	6	7
2	3	4	5	6	7	8	9	1
5	6	7	8	9	1	2	3	4
6	7	8	9	1	2	3	4	5
9	1	2	3	4	5	6	7	8

Let's continue.

Step 9	Fill **R9** with a circular shift of the sequence of numbers in **R8** by THREE slots.

In carrying out Step 9 above, we create a fully completed grid that now looks like this for Exercise 3.

Completed Practice Grid after Exercise "3R"

1	2	3	4	5	6	7	8	9
4	5	6	7	8	9	1	2	3
7	8	9	1	2	3	4	5	6
8	9	1	2	3	4	5	6	7
2	3	4	5	6	7	8	9	1
5	6	7	8	9	1	2	3	4
6	7	8	9	1	2	3	4	5
9	1	2	3	4	5	6	7	8
3	4	5	6	7	8	9	1	2

Congratulations to us! We have completed a grid using two different techniques: group filling BY ROW and circular shift.

Columns: an approach from a different angle ("3C")

Below is an example Step 1 for starting Exercise "3C."

Step 1	Fill C1 with nine different numbers **1**, **2**, **3**, **4**, **5**, **6**, **7**, **8**, **9**.

Note: We can fill C1 with any sequence
of nine different single digits.

After Step 1   *Exercise "3C"*

1								
2								
3								
4								
5								
6								
7								
8								
9								

Step 2	Fill **C2** with a circular shift of the sequence of numbers in **C1** by THREE slots.

After Step 2   Exercise "3C"

1	4							
2	5							
3	6							
4	7							
5	8							
6	9							
7	1							
8	2							
9	3							

Step 3	Fill **C3** with a circular shift of the sequence of numbers in **C2** by THREE slots.

After Step 3   Exercise "3C"

1	4	7						
2	5	8						
3	6	9						
4	7	1						
5	8	2						
6	9	3						
7	1	4						
8	2	5						
9	3	6						

Step 4	Fill **C4** with a circular shift of the sequence of numbers in **C3** by ONE slot.

After Step 4 *Exercise "3C"*

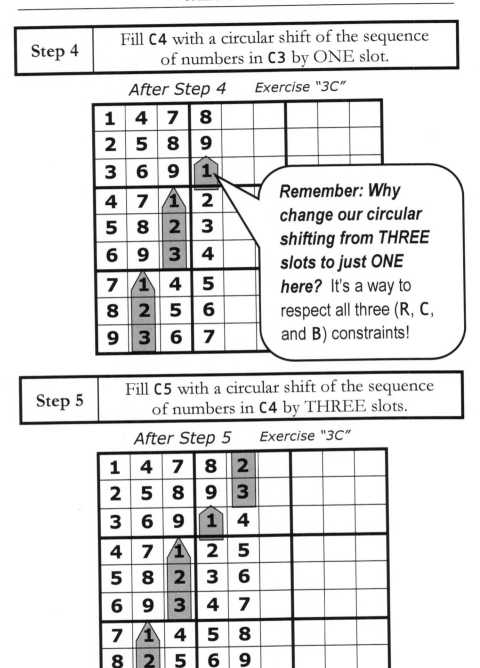

Remember: Why change our circular shifting from THREE slots to just ONE here? It's a way to respect all three (**R**, **C**, and **B**) constraints!

Step 5	Fill **C5** with a circular shift of the sequence of numbers in **C4** by THREE slots.

After Step 5 *Exercise "3C"*

Step 6	Fill **C6** with a circular shift of the sequence of numbers in **C5** by THREE slots.

After Step 6   Exercise "3C"

1	4	7	8	2	5			
2	5	8	9	3	6			
3	6	9	1	4	7			
4	7	1	2	5	8			
5	8	2	3	6	9			
6	9	3	4	7	1			
7	1	4	5	8	2			
8	2	5	6	9	3			
9	3	6	7	1	4			

Step 7	Fill **C7** with a circular shift of the sequence of numbers in **C6** by ONE slot.

After Step 7   Exercise "3C"

1	4	7	8	2	5	6		
2	5	8	9	3	6	7		
3	6	9	1	4	7	8		
4	7	1	2	5	8	9		
5	8	2	3	6	9	1		
6	9	3	4	7	1	2		
7	1	4	5	8	2	3		
8	2	5	6	9	3	4		
9	3	6	7	1	4	5		

Change from THREE slots to just ONE here to respect all three constraints!

Step 8	Fill **C8** with a circular shift of the sequence of numbers in **C7** by THREE slots.

After Step 8   *Exercise "3C"*

1	4	7	8	2	5	6	9	
2	5	8	9	3	6	7	1	
3	6	9	1	4	7	8	2	
4	7	1	2	5	8	9	3	
5	8	2	3	6	9	1	4	
6	9	3	4	7	1	2	5	
7	1	4	5	8	2	3	6	
8	2	5	6	9	3	4	7	
9	3	6	7	1	4	5	8	

Step 9	Fill **C9** with a circular shift of the sequence of numbers in **C8** by THREE slots.

Completed Practice Grid after Exercise "3C"

1	4	7	8	2	5	6	9	3
2	5	8	9	3	6	7	1	4
3	6	9	1	4	7	8	2	5
4	7	1	2	5	8	9	3	6
5	8	2	3	6	9	1	4	7
6	9	3	4	7	1	2	5	8
7	1	4	5	8	2	3	6	9
8	2	5	6	9	3	4	7	1
9	3	6	7	1	4	5	8	2

Thus we have completed a grid using both group filling BY COLUMN and circular shift.

Boxes round out our three approaches ("3BX")

Steps and grids that you'll see in a moment present another approach—group filling BY BOX plus circular-shift as before. But first, a short discussion about this particular group filling approach.

Note that we can fill **B1** with any sequence of nine different single digits. For the box sequence, read the sequence from left to right and top to bottom—same as we would read a book. For clarity, I will show how circular shifts work for boxes using the following example. I mark the **3**s with a gray background to make the patterns more noticeable.

Let us fill B1 with a sequence:
1 4 7
2 5 8
3 6 9
Which is: {**1, 4, 7, 2, 5, 8, 3, 6, 9**}

A circular shift of sequence B1 by ONE slot is:
4 7 2
5 8 3
6 9 1
Which is: {**4, 7, 2, 5, 8, 3, 6, 9, 1**}

A circular shift of sequence B1 by TWO slots is:

7 2 5
8 3 6
9 1 4

Which is: {**7, 2, 5, 8, 3, 6, 9**, 1, 4}

A circular shift of sequence B1 by THREE slots is:

2 5 8
3 6 9
1 4 7

Which is: {**2, 5, 8, 3, 6, 9, 1, 4, 7**}

Ready to continue? Let's do it.

	Fill **B1** with a sequence:
Step 1	**1 4 7** **2 5 8** **3 6 9**

After Step 1   *Exercise "3BX"*

1	4	7						
2	5	8						
3	6	9						

Step 2	Fill **B2** with a circular shift of the sequence of numbers in **B1** by THREE slots.

After Step 2   Exercise *"3BX"*

1	4	7	2	5	8			
2	5	8	3	6	9			
3	6	9	1	4	7			

Step 3	Fill **B3** with a circular shift of the sequence of numbers in **B2** by THREE slots.

After Step 3   Exercise *"3BX"*

1	4	7	2	5	8	3	6	9
2	5	8	3	6	9	1	4	7
3	6	9	1	4	7	2	5	8

Step 4	Fill **B4** with a circular shift of the sequence of numbers in **B3** by ONE slot.

After Step 4   Exercise "3BX"

Remember: We change our circular shifting from THREE slots to just ONE here to respect all three (R, C, and B) constraints!

Step 5	Fill **B5** with a circular shift of the sequence of numbers in **B4** by THREE slots.

After Step 5   Exercise "3BX"

Step 6	Fill **B6** with a circular shift of the sequence of numbers in **B5** by THREE slots.

After Step 6   Exercise "3BX"

1	4	7	2	5	8	3	6	9
2	5	8	3	6	9	1	4	7
3	6	9	1	4	7	2	5	8
6	9	1	4	7	2	5	8	3
4	7	2	5	8	3	6	9	1
5	8	3	6	9	1	4	7	2

Step 7	Fill **B7** with a circular shift of the sequence of numbers in **B6** by ONE slot.

After Step 7   Exercise "3BX"

1	4	7	2	5	8	3	6	9
2	5	8	3	6	9	1	4	7
3	6	9	1	4	7	2	5	8
6	9	1	4	7	2	5	8	3
4	7	2	5	8	3	6	9	1
5	8	3	6	9	1	4	7	2
8	3	6						
9	1	4						
7	2	5						

Change from THREE slots to just ONE here to respect all three constraints!

Step 8	Fill **B8** with a circular shift of the sequence of numbers in **B7** by THREE slots.

After Step 8   Exercise "3BX"

1	4	7	2	5	8	3	6	9
2	5	8	3	6	9	1	4	7
3	6	9	1	4	7	2	5	8
6	9	1	4	7	2	5	8	3
4	7	2	5	8	3	6	9	1
5	8	3	6	9	1	4	7	2
8	3	6	9	1	4			
9	1	4	7	2	5			
7	2	5	8	3	6			

Step 9	Fill **B9** with a circular shift of the sequence of numbers in **B8** by THREE slots.

Completed Practice Grid after Exercise "3BX"

1	4	7	2	5	8	3	6	9
2	5	8	3	6	9	1	4	7
3	6	9	1	4	7	2	5	8
6	9	1	4	7	2	5	8	3
4	7	2	5	8	3	6	9	1
5	8	3	6	9	1	4	7	2
8	3	6	9	1	4	7	2	5
9	1	4	7	2	5	8	3	6
7	2	5	8	3	6	9	1	4

Congratulations to us again! Through practice exercises "1," "2," "3R," "3C," and "3BX," we have learned how to fill grids in minutes using group filling and circular-shifting!

4 – VARIATIONS ON COMPLETED GRIDS

With a fully completed grid in our hands (from Chapter 3), we may OPTIONALLY apply variations. Before we start to remove numbers from the grid, explore these variations with me, five in all. The first four are easy. Apply them as you like to your own fully completed grids—and even to puzzles you have *finished setting*, think about it! The fifth variation, *Swaps*, will call for a bit of strategy, and you can apply swaps up front only, *before* removing any numbers.

Exchanges, rotations, flips, and diagonals

You may have noticed:

- We can exchange any two rows within row "trios" {R1, R2, R3} or {R4, R5, R6} or {R7, R8, R9}, and any two columns within columns "trios" {C1, C2, C3} or {C4, C5, C6} or {C7, C8, C9}.
- We can rotate a grid by 90, 180, or 270 degrees.
- We can flip a grid at R5 and/or C5, and D1 and/or D2! (We remember diagonals D1 and D2, don't we?)

Why this works: Exchanged, rotated, and/or flipped rows, columns, and boxes still distribute numbers **1** to **9** as required. Thus, all variations we choose will respect the row constraint, column constraint and box constraint.

In the cascade of examples that follow, read the captions and see for yourself how each variation works. Each grid is based on the one before it.

A Fully Completed Grid

Note: Use the gray squares to "spot" the variations.

1	4	7	2	5	8	3	6	9
2	5	8	3	6	9	1	4	7
3	6	9	1	4	7	2	5	8
6	9	1	4	7	2	5	8	3
4	7	2	5	8	3	6	9	1
5	8	3	6	9	1	4	7	2
8	3	6	9	1	4	7	2	5
9	1	4	7	2	5	8	3	6
7	2	5	8	3	6	9	1	4

Column-exchange: Moving C4 and C5

1	4	7	5	2	8	3	6	9
2	5	8	6	3	9	1	4	7
3	6	9	4	1	7	2	5	8
6	9	1	7	4	2	5	8	3
4	7	2	8	5	3	6	9	1
5	8	3	9	6	1	4	7	2
8	3	6	1	9	4	7	2	5
9	1	4	2	7	5	8	3	6
7	2	5	3	8	6	9	1	4

Row-exchange: Moving R1 and R2

2	5	8	6	3	9	1	4	7
1	4	7	5	2	8	3	6	9
3	6	9	4	1	7	2	5	8
6	9	1	7	4	2	5	8	3
4	7	2	8	5	3	6	9	1
5	8	3	9	6	1	4	7	2
8	3	6	1	9	4	7	2	5
9	1	4	2	7	5	8	3	6
7	2	5	3	8	6	9	1	4

Another Row-exchange: Moving R4 and R5

2	5	8	6	3	9	1	4	7
1	4	7	5	2	8	3	6	9
3	6	9	4	1	7	2	5	8
4	7	2	8	5	3	6	9	1
6	9	1	7	4	2	5	8	3
5	8	3	9	6	1	4	7	2
8	3	6	1	9	4	7	2	5
9	1	4	2	7	5	8	3	6
7	2	5	3	8	6	9	1	4

Note: Rows and columns exchanged need not be adjacent, just within the same column or row of mid-size boxes.

90° Rotation

C1 *from the previous grid* slides around to become a "backward" **R1**.

7	9	8	5	6	4	3	1	2
2	1	3	8	9	7	6	4	5
5	4	6	3	1	2	9	7	8
3	2	1	9	7	8	4	5	6
8	7	9	6	4	5	1	2	3
6	5	4	1	2	3	7	8	9
9	8	7	4	5	6	2	3	1
1	3	2	7	8	9	5	6	4
4	6	5	2	3	1	8	9	7

Spin along a Diagonal: D1

C9 *above* falls to the left like a tree (*"Timber!"*) to become **R9** *below*.

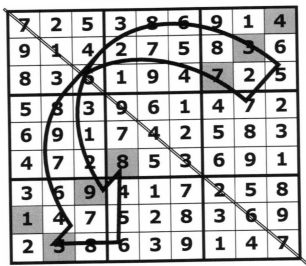

Note: We discussed diagonals earlier on page 6.

Swaps

You may have noticed: Our completed grids contain "frequent trios" that result from use of circular shifting along with group filling. OPTIONALLY, you may eliminate these "trio patterns" that puzzle-solvers could exploit. Swaps can scatter patterns. If you want to apply swaps, you must do so *before* removing any numbers!

- ***Box-Column (B-C) Swap:*** Columns trios side-by-side are swappable. (See examples inside **B7–B9** below.)

- ***Box-Row (B-R) Swap:*** Row trios above/below each other are swappable. (See non-swappable non-examples in **B1–B3** below: They are not above/below each other.)

Grid with Row Trios and Column Trios

7	2	5	3	8	6	9	1	4
9	1	4	2	7	5	8	3	6
8	3	6	1	9	4	7	2	5
5	8	3	9	6	1	4	7	2
6	9	1	7	4	2	5	8	3
4	7	2	8	5	3	6	9	1
3	6	9	4	1	7	2	5	8
1	4	7	5	2	8	3	6	9
2	5	8	6	3	9	1	4	7

Box-Row and Box-Column swaps

Study example grids that follow. Note underlined numbers within some of them. To achieve "impossible" **B-R** swaps, just precede them with well-chosen **B-C** swaps.

A B-C *Swap Prepares the Way for a* B-R *Swap*
B-C Swap1 (gray) + B-R Swap2 prep (underlines) BEFORE

7	2	5	3	8	6	9	1	4
9	1	4	2	7	5	8	3	6
8	**3**	**6**	1	9	4	7	2	5
5	**8**	**3**	9	**6**	1	4	7	2
6	9	1	7	**4**	2	5	8	3
4	7	2	8	**5**	3	6	9	1
3	6	9	4	1	7	2	5	8
1	4	7	5	2	8	3	6	9
2	5	8	6	3	9	1	4	7

The B-R *Swap Can Now Take Place*
B-C Swap1 AFTER (plain); B-R Swap2 (gray) BEFORE

7	2	5	3	8	6	9	1	4
9	1	4	2	7	5	8	3	6
8	3	6	1	9	4	7	2	5
6	8	3	9	5	1	4	7	2
4	9	1	7	6	2	5	8	3
5	7	2	8	4	3	6	9	1
3	6	9	4	1	7	2	5	8
1	4	7	5	2	8	3	6	9
2	5	8	6	3	9	1	4	7

To scatter pattern trios further, we may continue with additional strategic swaps. Here are more examples.

Another B-C *Swap Paves the Way for a* B-R *Swap*
B-R Swap2 AFTER (plain);
B-C Swap3 (gray) + B-R Swap4 prep (underlines) BEFORE

7	2	5	3	8	6	9	1	4
9	1	4	2	7	5	8	3	6
6	8	3	1	9	4	7	2	5
8	3	6	9	5	1	4	7	2
4	9	1	7	6	2	_5_	_8_	_3_
5	7	2	8	4	3	6	9	1
_3_	6	9	4	1	7	2	_5_	_8_
1	4	7	5	2	8	3	6	9
2	5	8	6	3	9	1	4	7

Another B-R *Swap*
B-C Swap3 AFTER (plain); B-R Swap4 (gray) BEFORE

7	2	5	3	8	6	9	1	4
9	1	4	2	7	5	8	3	6
6	8	3	1	9	4	7	2	5
8	3	6	9	5	1	4	7	2
4	9	1	7	6	2	5	8	3
5	7	2	8	4	3	6	9	1
2	6	9	4	1	7	3	5	8
3	4	7	5	2	8	1	6	9
1	5	8	6	3	9	2	4	7

A Third B-C Swap Paves the Way for a B-R Swap
B-R Swap4 AFTER (plain);
B-C Swap5 (gray) + B-R Swap6 prep (underlines) BEFORE

7	2	5	3	8	6	9	1	4
9	1	4	2	7	5	8	3	6
6	8	3	<u>1</u>	<u>9</u>	4	7	2	<u>5</u>
8	3	6	<u>9</u>	<u>5</u>	<u>1</u>	4	7	2
4	9	1	7	6	2	3	5	8
5	7	2	8	4	3	6	9	1
2	6	9	4	1	7	5	8	3
3	4	7	5	2	8	1	6	9
1	5	8	6	3	9	2	4	7

A Third B-R Swap
B-C Swap5 AFTER (plain); B-R Swap6 (gray) BEFORE

7	2	5	3	8	4	9	1	6
9	1	4	2	7	6	8	3	5
6	8	3	1	9	5	7	2	4
8	3	6	9	5	1	4	7	2
4	9	1	7	6	2	3	5	8
5	7	2	8	4	3	6	9	1
2	6	9	4	1	7	5	8	3
3	4	7	5	2	8	1	6	9
1	5	8	6	3	9	2	4	7

Status Snapshot
B-R Swap6 AFTER (plain);
Pattern trios are still seen in *B3*, *B7*, and *B8*.

7	2	5	3	8	4	9	1	6
9	1	4	2	7	6	8	3	5
6	8	3	9	5	1	7	2	4
8	3	6	1	9	5	4	7	2
4	9	1	7	6	2	3	5	8
5	7	2	8	4	3	6	9	1
2	6	9	4	1	7	5	8	3
3	4	7	5	2	8	1	6	9
1	5	8	6	3	9	2	4	7

To remove more pattern trios, we continue as follows.

A Double B-C Swap Paves the Way for One More
B-C Swap7/8 (gray) + B-R Swap9 prep (underl.) BEFORE

7	2	5	3	8	4	9	1	6
9	1	4	2	7	6	8	3	5
6	8	3	9	5	1	7	2	4
8	3	6	1	9	5	4	7	2
4	9	1	7	6	2	3	5	8
5	7	2	8	4	3	6	9	1
2	6	9	4	1	7	5	8	3
3	4	7	5	2	8	1	6	9
1	5	8	6	3	9	2	4	7

Note: B-C trios above swap R1 ⇆ R5, and R2 ⇆ R4.

Fourth and Final Example B-R Swap

B-C Swap7/8 AFTER (plain); B-R Swap9 (gray) BEFORE

7	2	5	3	8	4	9	1	6
9	1	4	2	7	6	8	3	5
6	8	3	9	5	1	7	2	4
8	3	6	1	9	5	4	7	2
4	9	1	7	6	2	3	5	8
5	7	2	8	4	3	6	9	1
1	4	9	6	2	7	5	8	3
2	5	7	4	3	8	1	6	9
3	6	8	5	1	9	2	4	7

Status Snapshot

B-R Swap9 AFTER (plain)

7	2	5	3	8	4	9	1	6
1	4	9	2	7	6	8	3	5
6	8	3	9	5	1	7	2	4
8	3	6	1	9	5	4	7	2
4	9	1	7	6	2	3	5	8
5	7	2	8	4	3	6	9	1
9	1	4	6	2	7	5	8	3
2	5	7	4	3	8	1	6	9
3	6	8	5	1	9	2	4	7

Pattern trios that remain in *B3* and *B8* are insignificant. We can stop here, or you may press on to scatter them also. (Hint: Just two easy B-R swaps will complete the task!)

5 – REMOVE NUMBERS

As you have seen, our basic approach to manually create a Sudoku puzzle is a two-stage process:

1. Make a fully completed grid using special techniques.
2. <u>Remove numbers from the grid.</u>

As we venture into the second stage, let us start with a an observation and an explanation. As *solvers*, we gradually *fill* our Sudoku grids with numbers. As *setters*, we apply solving in reverse. Both capabilities are powered by our depth of appreciation for logic. Though by no means is it required reading, I heartily recommend Peter Gordon's book, *Mensa Guide to Solving Sudoku* (2006), and its discussions of eleven *solving* techniques, ten which can apply to puzzling-setting. (The lone exception is Gordonian logic.)

- One-choice
- Elimination
- Scanning
- Subsets
- Interaction
- Gordonian logic
- Candidate-free solving
- The X-Wing family
- Forcing chains and grid coloring
- Bilocation and bivalue graphs
- Guessing

In keeping with the value proposition that you can "make your own in minutes," I focus on two techniques, One-choice and Elimination, first as used for solving and then as used for puzzle-setting, that is, removing numbers from our puzzle grids.

Getting to know "One-choice" and "Elimination"

As puzzle-solvers, we use One-choice when we discover that, for a specific empty square, only one still-available (unplaced) number can fit. All other numbers are seen at least once in the R–C–B areas of the square. Thus, the still-available number belongs in the square.

One-choice Technique to Fill R4C5

				3				
1		2				5		
					8			
				4				
				6				
				7				

A One-choice scenario: In R4C5, **9** must fit because:

- **1**, **2**, and **5** won't fit because of row constraint
- **3**, **4**, **6**, and **7** won't fit due to column constraint, and
- **4** and **8** won't fit thanks to box constraint.

As puzzle-solvers, we use Elimination when we discover that a still-available (unplaced) number has just one possible home within a specific **R** or **C** or **B**. Thus, we can place that still-available number accordingly.

Elimination of Options for *7* in *R7*

7								
	7							
✕		**1**	**2**	**3**	**4**	**5**	**6**	

An Elimination scenario: We remove **R7C1** and **R7C2** from consideration due to column constraint. Now with just one empty square remaining, the still-available (unplaced) number **7** can fit only in **R7C9**.

One-choice and Elimination for number removal

We have learned two basic techniques to solve a Sudoku puzzle as preparation for learning how to remove numbers from a fully completed or partially filled grid.

We remove numbers from our grid step-by-step, methodically. We won't remove too many numbers too fast. At most, we remove two numbers at a time to allow us to test whether a removal can be done *safely*.

Take care when a number removal test does NOT PASS. Unfortunately, we CANNOT "let it slide." Do NOT clear away numbers that do not pass tests. We need logic to back us up with every number removal!

What are the tests? How will they PASS?

Our tests are searches for clear support that solving techniques are available to our puzzle-solvers every step of the way. As puzzle-setters, we are working backwards, and we just need to focus on three items simultaneously. A test passes only if we can get logic's full cooperation. Which items require our simultaneous focus? (1.) The grid's *current* state in terms of cleared squares and filled squares—of course, the environment changes with every step! (2.) a specific square, and (3.) the number in it. Consider the solving technique scenarios presented just recently. In puzzle-setting mode (working backwards), as we aim to clear squares rather than fill them, and...

- As we study the *current One-Choice scenario* grid and square **R4C5**, we see the *current* R-C-B constraints show plainly that only **9** can fit this square *now*.

- As we study the *current Elimination scenario* grid and square **R7C9**, we see the *current* arrangement of other **7**s show plainly that only **7** can fit this square *now*.

Thus these tests PASS. We may be able to clear these squares. Why "may be able" and not "can"? Read on!

Choosing symmetrical pairs

Let's recall from Chapter 1: A classic Sudoku puzzle has pre-filled, symmetrical squares and when rotated 180 degrees, the same squares are pre-filled. We must keep symmetry in mind in order to make a classic Sudoku puzzle, which means we must be mindful of symmetry as we remove numbers from a grid. Example pairs of symmetrical squares include:

- **R1C1** and **R9C9**
- **R5C5** and **R5C5**
- **R3C7** and **R7C3**
- **R2C4** and **R8C6** *(See the pair of gray squares below.)*

Symmetrical Squares *R2C4* and *R8C6*

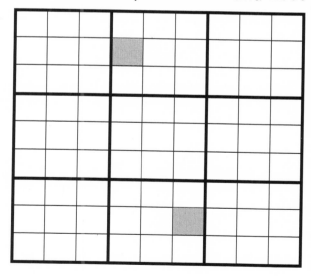

Puzzle-SETTING, puzzle-SOLVING: the difference?

For those of us who are ever curious to compare and contrast closely related topics: a brief Q&A session.

During puzzle-SETTING, for each square in the symmetrical pair, can its number be CLEARED safely? If at least one path to a correct inference is seen per square—let's not forget the pair—then YES.

Thus IF within the square's own R-C-B...

- all other (eight) numbers are seen at least one time, THEN its number remains inferable by *One-choice*, **OR**

- other cleared squares cannot possibly hold the number, THEN its number remains inferable by *Elimination*.

During puzzle-SOLVING, how do we know that a still-available number will correctly FILL a square? It is the correct choice if within the square's own R-C-B...

- all other (eight) numbers are seen at least one time, as indicative of *One-choice*, **OR**

- other empty squares cannot possibly hold one of the still-available numbers, as indicative of *Elimination*.

At any step, there are many pairs of symmetrical squares with pre-filled numbers. Suppose at one step, we have the following symmetrical squares with pre-filled numbers:

- Pair 1: **R1C1, R9C9**
- Pair 2: **R5C5, R5C5**
- Pair 3: **R4C6, R6C4**

We try Pair 1. If the numbers in these two squares are removed from the grid, can each square be inferred to contain one and only one number? If "Yes," then we can remove the numbers of Pair 1. If "No," then we try Pair 2, repeating the procedure. As you might already suspect, the first few rounds are easy, and challenges increase as we go.

Removing numbers, clearing squares: an example

Starting with a fully completed grid (taken from page 49), we will see step-by-step how to remove numbers in order to create a classic Sudoku puzzle.

A Fully Completed Grid

2	5	8	6	3	9	1	4	7
1	4	7	5	2	8	3	6	9
3	6	9	4	1	7	2	5	8
4	7	2	8	5	3	6	9	1
6	9	1	7	4	2	5	8	3
5	8	3	9	6	1	4	7	2
8	3	6	1	9	4	7	2	5
9	1	4	2	7	5	8	3	6
7	2	5	3	8	6	9	1	4

| Step 1 | Remove numbers from **R1C9** and **R9C1**. |

- At **R1C9**, **7** is inferable by *One-choice*.
  Any way you look at it, it becomes the only number not placed or seen within the contexts of **R1** *or* **C9** *or* **B3**.
- At **R9C1**, another **7** is inferable by *One-choice*.
  Any way you look at it, it becomes the only number not placed or seen within the contexts of **R9** *or* **C1** *or* **B7**.

Note: To pass a removal test,
just one support (supporting context) is sufficient.

For illustration purposes, I sometimes list *multiple* possible ways to find a PASS result, but
I do not attempt to list here all possible ways.

After Step 1: 2 Cleared Squares

2	5	8	6	3	9	1	4	
1	4	7	5	2	8	3	6	9
3	6	9	4	1	7	2	5	8
4	7	2	8	5	3	6	9	1
6	9	1	7	4	2	5	8	3
5	8	3	9	6	1	4	7	2
8	3	6	1	9	4	7	2	5
9	1	4	2	7	5	8	3	6
	2	5	3	8	6	9	1	4

Step 2	Remove numbers from **R2C6** and **R8C4**.

- At **R2C6**, **8** is inferable by *One-choice*.
  Any way you look at it, it becomes the only number not placed or seen within the contexts of **R2** *or* **C6** *or* **B2**.
- At **R8C4**, **2** is inferable by *One-choice*.
  Any way you look at it, it becomes the only number not placed or seen within the contexts of **R8** *or* **C4** *or* **B8**.

After Step 2: 4 Cleared Squares

2	5	8	6	3	9	1	4	
1	4	7	5	2		3	6	9
3	6	9	4	1	7	2	5	8
4	7	2	8	5	3	6	9	1
6	9	1	7	4	2	5	8	3
5	8	3	9	6	1	4	7	2
8	3	6	1	9	4	7	2	5
9	1	4		7	5	8	3	6
	2	5	3	8	6	9	1	4

Step 3	Remove numbers from **R3C6** and **R7C4**.

- At **R3C6**, **7** is inferable by *One-choice*.
  It becomes the only number not seen in **R3**.
- At **R7C4**, **1** is inferable by *One-choice*.
  It becomes the only number not seen in **R7**.

After Step 3: 6 Cleared Squares

2	5	8	6	3	9	1	4	
1	4	7	5	2		3	6	9
3	6	9	4	1		2	5	8
4	7	2	8	5	3	6	9	1
6	9	1	7	4	2	5	8	3
5	8	3	9	6	1	4	7	2
8	3	6		9	4	7	2	5
9	1	4		7	5	8	3	6
	2	5	3	8	6	9	1	4

Step 4	Remove numbers from **R4C3** and **R6C7**.

- At **R4C3**, **2** is inferable by *One-choice*.
  Any way you look at it, it becomes the only number not placed or seen within the contexts of **R4** *or* **C3** *or* **B4**.
- At **R6C7**, **4** is inferable by *One-choice*.
  Any way you look at it, it becomes the only number not placed or seen within the contexts of **R6** *or* **C7** *or* **B6**.

Reminder: To pass a removal test,
just one support (supporting context) is sufficient.

After Step 4: 8 Cleared Squares

2	5	8	6	3	9	1	4	
1	4	7	5	2		3	6	9
3	6	9	4	1		2	5	8
4	7		8	5	3	6	9	1
6	9	1	7	4	2	5	8	3
5	8	3	9	6	1		7	2
8	3	6		9	4	7	2	5
9	1	4		7	5	8	3	6
	2	5	3	8	6	9	1	4

Step 5	Remove number from **R5C5**.

- At **R5C5**, **4** is inferable by *One-choice*.
  Any way you look at it, it becomes the only number not placed or seen within the contexts of **R5** *or* **C5** *or* **B5**.

Note: Among the 81 squares,
R5C5 is the only square
whose symmetrical square is itself.

After Step 5: 9 Cleared Squares

2	5	8	6	3	9	1	4	
1	4	7	5	2		3	6	9
3	6	9	4	1		2	5	8
4	7		8	5	3	6	9	1
6	9	1	7		2	5	8	3
5	8	3	9	6	1		7	2
8	3	6		9	4	7	2	5
9	1	4		7	5	8	3	6
	2	5	3	8	6	9	1	4

| Step 6 | Remove numbers from **R1C1** and **R9C9**. |

- At **R1C1**, **2** is inferable by *One-choice*.
  It becomes the only number not seen within **B1**.
- At **R9C9**, **4** is inferable by *One-choice*.
  It becomes the only number not seen within **B9**.

After Step 6: 11 Cleared Squares

	5	8	6	3	9	1	4	
1	4	7	5	2		3	6	9
3	6	9	4	1		2	5	8
4	7		8	5	3	6	9	1
6	9	1	7		2	5	8	3
5	8	3	9	6	1		7	2
8	3	6		9	4	7	2	5
9	1	4		7	5	8	3	6
	2	5	3	8	6	9	1	

Step 7	Remove numbers from **R2C3** and **R8C7**.

- At **R2C3**, **7** is inferable by *One-choice*. It becomes the only number not seen within the combination of **R2** *and* **C3**.
- At **R8C7**, **8** is inferable by *One-choice*. It becomes the only number not seen within the combination of **R8** *and* **B9**.

After Step 7: 13 Cleared Squares

	5	8	6	3	9	1	4	
1	4	▓	5	2		3	6	9
3	6	9	4	1		2	5	8
4	7		8	5	3	6	9	1
6	9	1	7		2	5	8	3
5	8	3	9	6	1		7	2
8	3	6		9	4	7	2	5
9	1	4		7	5	▓	3	6
	2	5	3	8	6	9	1	

Step 8	Remove numbers from **R3C1** and **R7C9**.

- At **R3C1**, **3** is inferable by *Elimination*.

  In **B1**, other previously cleared squares cannot house **3**.
- At **R7C9**, **5** is inferable by *One-choice*.

  It becomes the only number not seen within the combination of **R7** *and* **C9**.

After Step 8: 15 Cleared Squares

	5	8	6	3	9	1	4	
1	4		5	2		3	6	9
	6	9	4	1		2	5	8
4	7		8	5	3	6	9	1
6	9	1	7		2	5	8	3
5	8	3	9	6	1		7	2
8	3	6		9	4	7	2	
9	1	4		7	5		3	6
	2	5	3	8	6	9	1	

| Step 9 | Remove numbers from **R4C8** and **R6C2**. |

- At **R4C8**, **9** is inferable by *One-choice*.
  It becomes the only number not seen within **C8**.
- At **R6C2**, **8** is inferable by *One-choice*.
  It becomes the only number not seen within **C2**.

After Step 9: 17 Cleared Squares

	5	8	6	3	9	1	4	
1	4		5	2		3	6	9
	6	9	4	1		2	5	8
4	7		8	5	3	6		1
6	9	1	7		2	5	8	3
5		3	9	6	1		7	2
8	3	6		9	4	7	2	
9	1	4		7	5		3	6
	2	5	3	8	6	9	1	

Step 10	Remove numbers from **R5C1** and **R5C9**.

- At **R5C1**, **6** is inferable by *One-choice*.
  It becomes the only number not seen within the combination of **R5** *and* **C1** *and* **B4**.
- At **R5C9**, **3** is inferable by *Elimination*.
  In **B6**, other previously cleared squares cannot house **3**.

After Step 10: 19 Cleared Squares

5	8	6	3	9		1	4	
1	4		5	2		3	6	9
	6	9	4	1		2	5	8
4	7		8	5	3	6		1
	9	1	7		2	5	8	
5		3	9	6	1		7	2
8	3	6		9	4	7	2	
9	1	4		7	5		3	6
	2	5	3	8	6	9	1	

| Step 11 | Remove numbers from **R2C8** and **R8C2**. |

- At **R2C8**, **6** is inferable by *One-choice*.
  It becomes the only number not seen within the combination of **C8** *and* **B3**.
- At **R8C2**, **1** is inferable by *One-choice*.
  It becomes the only number not seen within the combination of **R8** *and* **B7** (or also: **C2** *and* **B7**).

After Step 11: 21 Cleared Squares

	5	8	6	3	9	1	4	
1	4		5	2		3		9
	6	9	4	1		2	5	8
4	7		8	5	3	6		1
	9	1	7		2	5	8	
5		3	9	6	1		7	2
8	3	6		9	4	7	2	
9		4		7	5		3	6
	2	5	3	8	6	9	1	

Step 12	Remove numbers from **R3C7** and **R7C3**.

- At **R3C7**, **2** is inferable by *One-choice*.
  It becomes the only number not seen within the combination of **C7** *and* **B3**.
- At **R7C3**, **6** is inferable by *One-choice*.
  It becomes the only number not seen within the combination of **R7** *and* **C3**.

After Step 12: 23 Cleared Squares

	5	8	6	3	9		1	4	
1	4		5	2		3			9
	6	9	4	1				5	8
4	7		8	5	3	6			1
	9	1	7		2	5	8		
5		3	9	6	1			7	2
8	3			9	4	7	2		
9		4		7	5			3	6
	2	5	3	8	6	9	1		

Step 13	Remove numbers from **R2C5** and **R8C5**.

Note: Not all removal sequences are created equal. The sequence in which you clear squares may come into play in your logic strategy.

The first PASS result is possible only if the first test below occurs BEFORE the second test.

- At **R8C5**, **7** is inferable by *One-choice*. It becomes the only number not seen within the combination of **C5** *and* **B8**.
- At **R2C5**, **2** is inferable by *Elimination*. In **B2**, other previously cleared squares cannot house **2**.

After Step 13: 25 Cleared Squares

	5	8	6	3	9	1	4	
1	4		5			3		9
	6	9	4	1			5	8
4	7		8	5	3	6		1
	9	1	7		2	5	8	
5		3	9	6	1		7	2
8	3			9	4	7	2	
9		4			5		3	6
	2	5	3	8	6	9	1	

Step 14	Remove numbers from **R3C4** and **R7C6**.

Reminder: You can use sequence to your advantage: The first test below yields a PASS result only if conducted first.

- At **R3C4**, **4** is inferable by *Elimination*.
  In **B2**, other previously cleared squares cannot house **2**.
- At **R7C6**, another **4** is inferable by *One-choice*.
  It becomes the only number not seen within the combination of **R7** *and* **C6**.

After Step 14: 27 Cleared Squares

	5	8	6	3	9	1	4	
1	4		5			3		9
	6	9		1			5	8
4	7		8	5	3	6		1
	9	1	7		2	5	8	
5		3	9	6	1		7	2
8	3			9		7	2	
9		4			5		3	6
	2	5	3	8	6	9	1	

| Step 15 | Remove numbers from **R4C9** and **R6C1**. |

- At **R4C9**, **1** is inferable by *One-choice*.
  It becomes the only number not seen within the combination of **R4** *and* **C9**.
- At **R6C1**, **5** is inferable by *One-choice*.
  It becomes the only number not seen within the combination of **R6** *and* **C1**.

After Step 15: 29 Cleared Squares

	5	8	6	3	9	1	4	
1	4		5			3		9
	6	9		1			5	8
4	7		8	5	3	6		
	9	1	7		2	5	8	
		3	9	6	1		7	2
8	3			9		7	2	
9		4			5		3	6
	2	5	3	8	6	9	1	

After Step 15, the challenge heats up to find pairs that qualify for safe removal. Try this: Check how often numbers appear in the current grid. With 29 squares cleared, this grid's tally starts out like this.

1 ← 6 times   **2** ← 4 times   **3** ← 7 times! ...

Seven instances of **3** are still in the grid, so let's focus on where **3**s are. Let's test **R9C4**. PASS! Let's keep going!

Step 16	Remove numbers from **R9C4** and **R1C6**.

- At **R9C4**, **3** is inferable by *Elimination*.

   In **B8**, other previously cleared squares cannot house **3**.

- At **R1C6**, **9** is inferable by *Elimination*.

   In **B2**, other previously cleared squares cannot house **9**.

After Step 16: 31 Cleared Squares

	5	8	6	3		1	4	
1	4		5			3		9
	6	9		1			5	8
4	7		8	5	3	6		
	9	1	7		2	5	8	
		3	9	6	1		7	2
8	3			9		7	2	
9		4			5		3	6
	2	5		8	6	9	1	

Our example grid above now has 31 blank squares. Puzzle-solvers may have an easy time completing the grid because we used just two techniques—One-choice and Elimination. It might work as a beginner-level Sudoku in a newspaper or magazine. Try this if you like: Carefully remove more numbers from the grid to increase this puzzle's challenge level.

6 – A START-TO-FINISH EXAMPLE

This example takes us through both stages (1) "Make a fully completed grid using special techniques" and (2) "Remove numbers from the grid." Ready?

Start-to-finish: Stage 1—Making a fully completed grid

Step 1	Fill **B1** with this sequence: **9 2 5** **3 8 7** **6 4 1**

Fill **B1**

9	2	5						
3	8	7						
6	4	1						

| Step 2 | Fill **B2** with a circular shift of the sequence of numbers in **B1** by THREE slots. |

Fill B2

9	2	5	3	8	7			
3	8	7	6	4	1			
6	4	1	9	2	5			

| Step 3 | Fill **B3** with a circular shift of the sequence of numbers in **B2** by THREE slots. |

Fill B3

9	2	5	3	8	7	6	4	1
3	8	7	6	4	1	9	2	5
6	4	1	9	2	5	3	8	7

Step 4	Fill **B4** with a circular shift of the sequence of numbers in **B3** by ONE slot.

Fill B4

9	2	5	3	8	7	6	4	1
3	8	7	6	4	1	9	2	5
6	4	1	9	2	5	3	8	7
4	1	9						
2	5	3						
8	7	6						

Step 5	Fill **B5** with a circular shift of the sequence of numbers in **B4** by THREE slots.

Fill B5

9	2	5	3	8	7	6	4	1
3	8	7	6	4	1	9	2	5
6	4	1	9	2	5	3	8	7
4	1	9	2	5	3			
2	5	3	8	7	6			
8	7	6	4	1	9			

| Step 6 | Fill **B6** with a circular shift of the sequence of numbers in **B5** by THREE slots. |

Fill B6

9	2	5	3	8	7	6	4	1
3	8	7	6	4	1	9	2	5
6	4	1	9	2	5	3	8	7
4	1	9	2	5	3	8	7	6
2	5	3	8	7	6	4	1	9
8	7	6	4	1	9	2	5	3

| Step 7 | Fill **B7** with a circular shift of the sequence of numbers in **B6** by ONE slot. |

Fill B7

9	2	5	3	8	7	6	4	1
3	8	7	6	4	1	9	2	5
6	4	1	9	2	5	3	8	7
4	1	9	2	5	3	8	7	6
2	5	3	8	7	6	4	1	9
8	7	6	4	1	9	2	5	3
7	6	4						
1	9	2						
5	3	8						

Step 8	Fill **B8** with a circular shift of the sequence of numbers in **B7** by THREE slots.

Fill B8

9	2	5	3	8	7	6	4	1
3	8	7	6	4	1	9	2	5
6	4	1	9	2	5	3	8	7
4	1	9	2	5	3	8	7	6
2	5	3	8	7	6	4	1	9
8	7	6	4	1	9	2	5	3
7	6	4	1	9	2			
1	9	2	5	3	8			
5	3	8	7	6	4			

Step 9	Fill **B9** with a circular shift of the sequence of numbers in **B8** by THREE slots.

Fill B9

9	2	5	3	8	7	6	4	1
3	8	7	6	4	1	9	2	5
6	4	1	9	2	5	3	8	7
4	1	9	2	5	3	8	7	6
2	5	3	8	7	6	4	1	9
8	7	6	4	1	9	2	5	3
7	6	4	1	9	2	5	3	8
1	9	2	5	3	8	7	6	4
5	3	8	7	6	4	1	9	2

| Step 10 | *It is optional to apply one or more variations.*
 Optional: Exchange **C4** and **C6**. |

Applying a variation: Swap columns within B2–B5–B8

9	2	5	7	8	3	6	4	1
3	8	7	1	4	6	9	2	5
6	4	1	5	2	9	3	8	
4	1	9	3	5	2	8	7	
2	5	3	6	7	8	4	1	
8	7	6	9	1	4	2		
7	6	4	2	9	1	5	3	8
1	9	2	8	3	5	7	6	4
5	3	8	4	6	7	1	9	2

> Columns need not be adjacent, but **must be** within the same column of mid-

| Step 11 | **Optional:** Exchange R4 and R6. |

Applying a variation: Swap rows within B4–B5–B6

9								
3								
6								
8	7	6	9	1	4	2	5	3
2	5	3	6	7	8	4	1	9
4	1	9	3	5	2	8	7	6
7	6	4	2	9	1	5	3	8
1	9	2	8	3	5	7	6	4
5	3	8	4	6	7	1	9	2

> Likewise, rows need not be adjacent, but in order to exchange one with the other, both **must be** within the same row of mid-size boxes.

Step 12	**Optional:** Swap column trios **B4C1** and **B5C6** in order to enable the <u>B–R swap</u> that follows.

Scattering trio patterns: A box-column swap

9	2	5	7	8	3	6	4	1
3	8	7	1	4	6	9	2	5
6	4	1	5	2	9	3	8	7
8	<u>7</u>	<u>6</u>	9	1	<u>4</u>	2	5	3
2	5	3	6	7	8	4	1	9
4	1	9	3	5	2	8	7	6
<u>7</u>	<u>6</u>	<u>4</u>	2	9	1	5	3	8
1	9	2	8	3	5	7	6	4
5	3	8	4	6	7	1	9	2

Step 13	**Optional:** Swap row trios **B4R4** and **B7R7**.

Scattering trio patterns: A box-row swap

9	2	5	7	8	3	6	4	1
3	8	7	1	4	6	9	2	5
6	4	1	5	2	9	3	8	7
4	7	6	9	1	8	2	5	3
8	5	3	6	7	2	4	1	9
2	1	9	3	5	4	8	7	6
7	6	4	2	9	1	5	3	8
1	9	2	8	3	5	7	6	4
5	3	8	4	6	7	1	9	2

Step 14	**Optional:** Swap column trios **B8C6** and **B9C7** in order to enable the <u>B–R swap</u> that follows.

Scattering trio patterns: A box-column swap

9	2	5	7	8	3	6	4	1
3	8	7	1	4	6	9	2	5
6	4	1	<u>5</u>	<u>2</u>	<u>9</u>	3	8	7
7	6	4	9	1	8	2	5	3
8	5	3	6	7	2	4	1	9
2	1	9	3	5	4	8	7	6
4	7	6	<u>2</u>	<u>9</u>	1	<u>5</u>	3	8
1	9	2	8	3	5	7	6	4
5	3	8	4	6	7	1	9	2

Step 15	**Optional:** Swap row trios **B2R3** and **B8R7**.

Scattering trio patterns: A box-row swap

9	2	5	7	8	3	6	4	1
3	8	7	1	4	6	9	2	5
6	4	1	5	2	9	3	8	7
7	6	4	9	1	8	2	5	3
8	5	3	6	7	2	4	1	9
2	1	9	3	5	4	8	7	6
4	7	6	2	9	5	1	3	8
1	9	2	8	3	7	5	6	4
5	3	8	4	6	1	7	9	2

Step 16	**Optional:** Swap column trios **B1C1** and **B3C7** in order to enable the <u>B–R swap</u> that follows.

Scattering trio patterns: A box-column swap

9	2	5	7	8	3	6	4	1
3	8	7	1	4	6	9	2	5
<u>6</u>	4	1	2	9	5	3	<u>8</u>	<u>7</u>
7	6	4	9	1	8	2	5	3
8	5	3	6	7	2	4	1	9
2	1	9	3	5	4	<u>8</u>	<u>7</u>	<u>6</u>
4	7	6	5	2	9	1	3	8
1	9	2	8	3	7	5	6	4
5	3	8	4	6	1	7	9	2

Step 17	**Optional:** Swap row trios **B3R3** and **B6R6**.

Scattering trio patterns: A box-row swap

6	2	5	7	8	3	9	4	1
9	8	7	1	4	6	3	2	5
3	4	1	2	9	5	6	8	7
7	6	4	9	1	8	2	5	3
8	5	3	6	7	2	4	1	9
2	1	9	3	5	4	8	7	6
4	7	6	5	2	9	1	3	8
1	9	2	8	3	7	5	6	4
5	3	8	4	6	1	7	9	2

Step 18	**Optional:** Check if pattern trios are now largely unnoticeable.

Pattern Trios Remaining?

6	2	5	7	8	3	9	4	1
9	8	7	1	4	6	3	2	5
3	4	1	2	9	5	8	7	6
7	6	4	9	1	8	2	5	3
8	5	3	6	7	2	4	1	9
2	1	9	3	5	4	6	8	7
4	7	6	5	2	9	1	3	8
1	9	2	8	3	7	5	6	4
5	3	8	4	6	1	7	9	2

At this point in our start-to-finish example, we have created a completely filled grid and applied variations in order to scatter pattern trios. Let's continue with the second stage.

Start-to-finish: Stage 2—Removing numbers

Step 19	Remove numbers from R1C1 and R9C9.

- At **R1C1, 6** is easily inferable. It becomes the only number unseen in **R1** *or* **C1** *or* **B1**. (*One-choice*)
- At **R9C9, 2** is easily inferable. It becomes the only number unseen in **R9** *or* **C9** *or* **B9**. (*One-choice*)

After Clearing 2 Squares

	2	5	7	8	3	9	4	1
9	8	7	1	4	6	3	2	5
3	4	1	2	9	5	8	7	6
7	6	4	9	1	8	2	5	3
8	5	3	6	7	2	4	1	9
2	1	9	3	5	4	6	8	7
4	7	6	5	2	9	1	3	8
1	9	2	8	3	7	5	6	4
5	3	8	4	6	1	7	9	

| Step 20 | Remove numbers from **R2C9** and **R8C1**. |

- At **R2C9**, **5** is easily inferable. It becomes the only number unseen in **R2** *or* **B3**. (*One-choice*)
- At **R8C1**, **1** is easily inferable. It becomes the only number unseen in **R8** *or* **B7**. (*One-choice*)

After Clearing 4 Squares

	2	5	7	8	3	9	4	1
9	8	7	1	4	6	3	2	
3	4	1	2	9	5	8	7	6
7	6	4	9	1	8	2	5	3
8	5	3	6	7	2	4	1	9
2	1	9	3	5	4	6	8	7
4	7	6	5	2	9	1	3	8
	9	2	8	3	7	5	6	4
5	3	8	4	6	1	7	9	

Step 21	Remove numbers from **R3C3** and **R7C7**.

- At **R3C3**, **1** is easily inferable. It becomes the only number unseen in **R3** *or* **C3**. (*One-choice*)
- At **R7C7**, another **1** is easily inferable. It becomes the only number unseen in **R7** *or* **C7**. (*One-choice*)

After Clearing 6 Squares

	2	5	7	8	3	9	4	1
9	8	7	1	4	6	3	2	
3	4	▨	2	9	5	8	7	6
7	6	4	9	1	8	2	5	3
8	5	3	6	7	2	4	1	9
2	1	9	3	5	4	6	8	7
4	7	6	5	2	9	▨	3	8
	9	2	8	3	7	5	6	4
5	3	8	4	6	1	7	9	

| Step 22 | Remove numbers from **R4C3** and **R6C7**. |

- At **R4C3**, **4** is easily inferable. It becomes the only number unseen in **R4** *or* **B4**. (*One-choice*)
- At **R6C7**, **6** is easily inferable. It becomes the only number unseen in **R6** *or* **B6**. (*One-choice*)

After Clearing 8 Squares

	2	5	7	8	3	9	4	1
9	8	7	1	4	6	3	2	
3	4		2	9	5	8	7	6
7	6		9	1	8	2	5	3
8	5	3	6	7	2	4	1	9
2	1	9	3	5	4		8	7
4	7	6	5	2	9		3	8
	9	2	8	3	7	5	6	4
5	3	8	4	6	1	7	9	

Step 23	Remove numbers from **R5C1** and **R5C9**.

- At **R5C1**, **8** is inferable.
  It won't fit in **B4**'s other cleared square. *(Elimination)*
- At **R5C9**, **9** is inferable.
  It won't fit in **B6**'s other cleared square. *(Elimination)*

After Clearing 10 Squares

	2	5	7	8	3	9	4	1
9	8	7	1	4	6	3	2	
3	4		2	9	5	8	7	6
7	6		9	1	8	2	5	3
	5	3	6	7	2	4	1	
2	1	9	3	5	4		8	7
4	7	6	5	2	9		3	8
	9	2	8	3	7	5	6	4
5	3	8	4	6	1	7	9	

Step 24	Remove numbers from **R1C4** and **R9C6**.

- At **R1C4**, **7** is easily inferable. It becomes the only number unseen in **C4** *or* **B2**. (*One-choice*)
- At **R9C6**, **1** is easily inferable. It becomes the only number unseen in **C6** *or* **B8**. (*One-choice*)

After Clearing 12 Squares

	2	5		8	3	9	4	1
9	8	7	1	4	6	3	2	
3	4		2	9	5	8	7	6
7	6		9	1	8	2	5	3
	5	3	6	7	2	4	1	
2	1	9	3	5	4		8	7
4	7	6	5	2	9		3	8
	9	2	8	3	7	5	6	4
5	3	8	4	6		7	9	

| **Step 25** | Remove numbers from **R1C9** and **R9C1**. |

- At **R1C9**, **1** is easily inferable.
  It won't fit in **B3**'s other cleared square. (*Elimination*)
- At **R9C1**, **5** is easily inferable.
  It won't fit in **B7**'s other cleared square. (*Elimination*)

After Clearing 14 Squares

	2	5		8	3	9	4	
9	8	7	1	4	6	3	2	
3	4		2	9	5	8	7	6
7	6		9	1	8	2	5	3
	5	3	6	7	2	4	1	
2	1	9	3	5	4		8	7
4	7	6	5	2	9		3	8
	9	2	8	3	7	5	6	4
	3	8	4	6		7	9	

| Step 26 | Remove numbers from **R4C9** and **R6C1**. |

- At **R4C9**, **3** is easily inferable.
  It won't fit in **R4**'s other cleared square. (*Elimination*)
- At **R6C1**, **2** is easily inferable.
  It won't fit in **R6**'s other cleared square. (*Elimination*)

After Clearing 16 Squares

	2	5		8	3	9	4	
9	8	7	1	4	6	3	2	
3	4		2	9	5	8	7	6
7	6		9	1	8	2	5	
	5	3	6	7	2	4	1	
	1	9	3	5	4		8	7
4	7	6	5	2	9		3	8
	9	2	8	3	7	5	6	4
	3	8	4	6		7	9	

| Step 27 | Remove numbers from **R1C8** and **R9C2**. |

- At **R1C8**, **4** is inferable.

  It becomes the only number unseen in **C8** *(One-choice)*.
- At **R9C2**, **3** is inferable.

  It becomes the only number unseen in **C2** *(One-choice)*.

After Clearing 18 Squares

	2	5		8	3	9		
9	8	7	1	4	6	3	2	
3	4		2	9	5	8	7	6
7	6		9	1	8	2	5	
	5	3	6	7	2	4	1	
	1	9	3	5	4		8	7
4	7	6	5	2	9		3	8
	9	2	8	3	7	5	6	4
		8	4	6		7	9	

Step 28	Remove numbers from **R1C2** and **R9C8**.

- At **R1C2**, **2** is inferable. It becomes the only number unseen in a combination of **C2** and **B1**. (*One-choice*)
- At **R9C8**, **9** is inferable.
  It won't fit in **C8**'s other cleared square. (*Elimination*)

After Clearing 20 Squares

		5		8	3	9		
9	8	7	1	4	6	3	2	
3	4		2	9	5	8	7	6
7	6		9	1	8	2	5	
	5	3	6	7	2	4	1	
	1	9	3	5	4		8	7
4	7	6	5	2	9		3	8
	9	2	8	3	7	5	6	4
		8	4	6		7		

Step 29	Remove numbers from **R1C7** and **R9C3**.

- At **R1C7**, **9** is inferable.
  It won't fit in **C7**'s other cleared squares. (*Elimination*)
- At **R9C3**, **8** is inferable.
  It won't fit in **C3**'s other cleared squares. (*Elimination*)

After Clearing 22 Squares

		5		8	3			
9	8	7	1	4	6	3	2	
3	4		2	9	5	8	7	6
7	6		9	1	8	2	5	
	5	3	6	7	2	4	1	
	1	9	3	5	4		8	7
4	7	6	5	2	9		3	8
	9	2	8	3	7	5	6	4
			4	6		7		

Step 30	Remove numbers from **R2C1** and **R8C9**.

- At **R2C1**, **9** is inferable. It is the only number unseen in a combination of **B1** and **R2**. (*One-choice*)
- At **R8C9**, **4** is inferable.
  It won't fit in **R8**'s other cleared square. (*Elimination*)

After Clearing 24 Squares

		5		8	3			
	8	7	1	4	6	3	2	
3	4		2	9	5	8	7	6
7	6		9	1	8	2	5	
	5	3	6	7	2	4	1	
	1	9	3	5	4		8	7
4	7	6	5	2	9		3	8
	9	2	8	3	7	5	6	
			4	6		7		

Step 31	Remove numbers from R2C6 and R8C4.

- At **R2C6**, **6** is easily inferable. It won't fit in **B2**'s other cleared square. (*Elimination*)
- At **R8C4**, **8** is easily inferable. It won't fit in **C4**'s other cleared square. (*Elimination*)

After Clearing 26 Squares

		5	8	3				
	8	7	1	4	▓	3	2	
3	4		2	9	5	8	7	6
7	6		9	1	8	2	5	
	5	3	6	7	2	4	1	
	1	9	3	5	4		8	7
4	7	6	5	2	9		3	8
	9	2	▓	3	7	5	6	
			4	6		7		

Step 32	Remove numbers from **R3C9** and **R7C1**.

- At **R3C9**, **6** is inferable.
  It won't fit in **R3**'s other cleared square. (*Elimination*)
- At **R7C1**, **4** is inferable.
  It won't fit in **R7**'s other cleared square. (*Elimination*)

After Clearing 28 Squares

		5		8	3			
	8	7	1	4		3	2	
3	4		2	9	5	8	7	
7	6		9	1	8	2	5	
	5	3	6	7	2	4	1	
	1	9	3	5	4		8	7
	7	6	5	2	9		3	8
	9	2		3	7	5	6	
			4	6		7		

Step 33	Remove numbers from **R3C8** and **R7C2**.

- At **R3C8**, **7** is inferable.
  It won't fit in **R3**'s other cleared squares. (*Elimination*)
- At **R7C2**, another **7** is inferable.
  It won't fit in **R7**'s other cleared squares. (*Elimination*)

After Clearing 30 Squares

		5		8	3			
	8	7	1	4		3	2	
3	4		2	9	5	8	▓	
7	6		9	1	8	2	5	
	5	3	6	7	2	4	1	
	1	9	3	5	4		8	7
	▓	6	5	2	9		3	8
	9	2		3	7	5	6	
			4	6		7		

Step 34	Remove numbers from **R4C5** and **R6C5**.

- At **R4C5**, **1** is inferable.
  It is the only number unseen in **B5**. (*One-choice*)
- At **R6C5**, **5** is inferable.
  It won't fit in **B5**'s other cleared square. (*Elimination*)

After Clearing 32 Squares

	5		8	3				
8	7	1	4		3	2		
3	4		2	9	5	8		
7	6		9	░	8	2	5	
5	3	6	7	2	4	1		
1	9	3	░	4		8	7	
	6	5	2	9		3	8	
9	2		3	7	5	6		
		4	6		7			

Step 35	Remove numbers from **R3C5** and **R7C5**.

- At **R3C5**, **9** is inferable.
  It won't fit in **C5**'s other cleared squares. (*Elimination*)
- At **R7C5**, **2** is inferable.
  It won't fit in **B8**'s other cleared squares. (*Elimination*)

After Clearing 34 Squares

		5		8	3			
	8	7	1	4		3	2	
3	4		2	▓	5	8		
7	6		9		8	2	5	
	5	3	6	7	2	4	1	
	1	9	3		4		8	7
		6	5	▓	9		3	8
	9	2		3	7	5	6	
			4	6		7		

| Step 36 | Remove numbers from **R5C6** and **R5C4**. |

Note: Not all removal sequences are created equal. The sequence in which you clear squares may come into play in your logic strategy.

The first PASS result is possible only if the first test below occurs BEFORE the second test.

- At **R5C6**, **2** is inferable. In **R5** and **C6** together, this is the only number unseen. *(One-choice)*
- At **R5C4**, **6** is inferable. In **C4** and **B5** together, this is the only number unseen. *(One-choice)*

After Clearing 36 Squares

		5		8	3			
	8	7	1	4		3	2	
3	4		2		5	8		
7	6		9		8	2	5	
	5	3		7		4	1	
	1	9	3		4		8	7
		6	5		9		3	8
	9	2		3	7	5	6	
			4	6		7		

Step 37	Remove numbers from R2C3 and R8C7.

- At **R2C3**, **7** is inferable. In **R2**, **C3**, and **B1** together, this is the only number not seen. (*One-choice*)
- At **R8C7**, **5** is inferable.
  It won't fit in **C7**'s other cleared squares. (*Elimination*)

After Clearing 38 Squares

		5		8	3			
	8		1	4		3	2	
3	4		2		5	8		
7	6		9		8	2	5	
	5	3		7		4	1	
	1	9	3		4		8	7
		6	5		9		3	8
	9	2		3	7		6	
			4	6		7		

Step 38	Remove number from **R4C2** and **R6C8**.

- At **R4C2**, **6** is inferable. In **R4**, **C2**, and **B4** together, this is the only number unseen. (*One-choice*)
- At **R6C8**, **8** is inferable.
  It won't fit in **C8**'s other cleared squares. (*Elimination*)

After Clearing 40 Squares

		5	8	3				
	8		1	4		3	2	
3	4		2		5	8		
7	▓		9		8	2	5	
	5	3		7		4	1	
	1	9	3		4		▓	7
		6	5		9		3	8
	9	2		3	7		6	
			4	6		7		

Now we have successfully cleared 40 squares from the fully completed grid—almost half the total of 81. The partially filled grid above is a manually created classic Sudoku.

Before presenting this Sudoku puzzle to family or friends, double-check whether you can solve it. Use One-choice, Elimination, and other techniques that you have learned or discovered.

| Step 39 | Check whether the created Sudoku puzzle has one, and only one, solution. |

Let's solve the manually created Sudoku.

At...	Fill in...	As allowed by method...	Step
R6C8	8	*Elimination* in C8	38
R4C2	6	*One-choice*	
R8C7	5	*Elimination* in C7	37
R2C3	7	*One-choice*	
R5C4	6	*One-choice*	36
R5C6	2	*One-choice*	
R7C5	2	*Elimination* in B8	35
R3C5	9	*Elimination* in C5	
R6C5	5	*Elimination* in B5	34
R4C5	1	*One-choice*	
R7C2	7	*Elimination* in R7	33
R3C8	7	*Elimination* in R3	
R7C1	4	*Elimination* in R7	32
R3C9	6	*Elimination* in R3	
R8C4	8	*Elimination* in C4	31
R2C6	6	*Elimination* in B2	
R8C9	4	*Elimination* in R8	30
R2C1	9	*One-choice*	
R9C3	8	*Elimination* in C3	29
R1C7	9	*Elimination* in C7	
R9C8	9	*Elimination* in C8	28
R1C2	2	*One-choice*	
R9C2	3	*One-choice*	27
R1C8	4	*One-choice*	
R6C1	2	*Elimination* in R6	26
R4C9	3	*Elimination* in R4	
R9C1	5	*Elimination* in B7	25
R1C9	1	*Elimination* in B3	

At...	Fill in...	As allowed by method...	Step
R9C6	**1**	*One-choice*	**24**
R1C4	**7**	*One-choice*	
R5C9	**9**	*Elimination* in B6	**23**
R5C1	**8**	*Elimination* in B4	

We have not yet finished but have you noticed?
Puzzle-solving is easier as we start and as we finish. It's most challenging in the middle. Near the finish, a puzzle may just melt into a series of *One-choice* fill-ins. This puzzle is that way: Only *One-choice* fill-ins remain, namely these.

At...	Fill in...	Step
R6C7	**6**	**22**
R4C3	**4**	
R7C7	**1**	**21**
R3C3	**1**	

At...	Fill in...	Step
R8C1	**1**	**20**
R2C9	**5**	
R9C9	**2**	**19**
R1C1	**6**	

Note: 41 still-filled squares + 40 squares above = 81.

So is it classic?

The steps in the table above show that this manually created Sudoku puzzle has just one and only one solution. Now check whether it exhibits 180-degree rotational symmetry. It does? Great! So congratulations to you! Now you have learned the basics to hand-craft classic Sudoku puzzles in minutes!

Try to continue clearing squares from this puzzle by carefully removing more numbers using the approaches that I have shown you.

Now you are ready to create your own!

With practice, you will craft interesting puzzles in an impressively short time. Share your classic Sudoku creations with family and friends!

And of course, as time passes and naturally you clear your mind about how you created your first puzzles, you can try to solve those all over again!

For your convenience, pages that follow hold blank grids. Use them to start to explore your new skills.

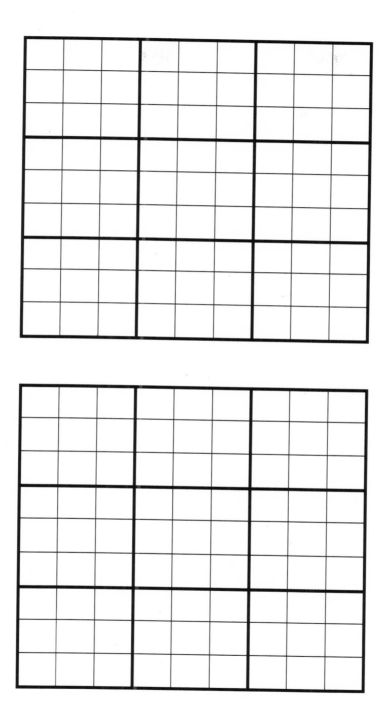

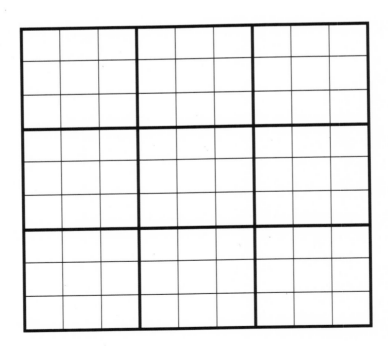

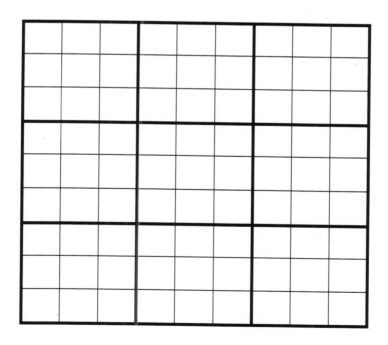

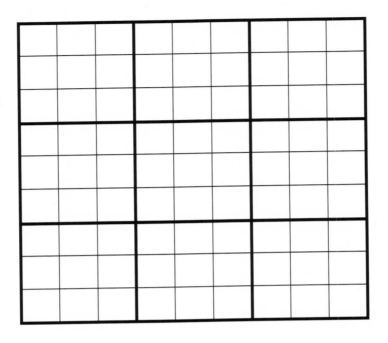

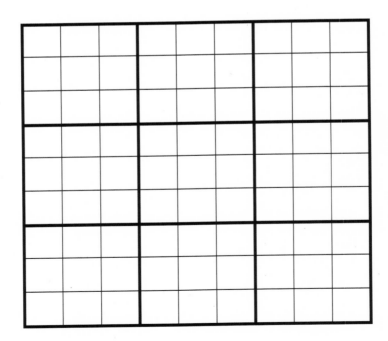

ABOUT THE AUTHOR

Dr. Yaling Zheng developed an interest in classic Sudoku puzzles while studying Constraint Satisfaction Problems (CSPs) at the University of Nebraska. With a focus on the Sudoku puzzle as a classic CSP, she designed an algorithm to enable computers to generate Sudoku puzzles within three seconds.

Then she wondered: Might mere mortals generate Sudoku puzzles without a computer's help, in a true do-it-yourself manner? She discovered that the goal *is* humanly achievable, it may take longer than three seconds but certainly within a humanly reasonable amount of time.

Thorough investigations led to some techniques and methods that allow just about anyone to proceed along a sure and steady path to hand-craft a classic Sudoku within minutes.

She hopes this book will spark your creative thinking and increase your enthusiasm for logical reasoning as you master the craft of a Sudoku puzzle-setter.

Visit www.createclassicsudoku.com for updates on her future work on this subject and to share your suggestions and comments!

Made in the USA
Middletown, DE
02 April 2019